THE NEW MEASURES

THE NEW MEASURES

Poems by

A. F. MORITZ

ANANSI

This edition published in 2012 by
House of Anansi Press Inc.
110 Spadina Avenue, Suite 801
Toronto, ON, M5V 2K4
Tel. 416-363-4343
Fax 416-363-1017
www.houseofanansi.com

Distributed in Canada by
HarperCollins Canada Ltd.
1995 Markham Road
Scarborough, ON, M1B 5M8
Toll-free tel. 1-800-387-0117

Distributed in the United States by
Publishers Group West
1700 Fourth Street
Berkeley, CA 94710
Toll-free tel. 1-800-788-3123

House of Anansi Press is committed to protecting our natural environment.
As part of our efforts, the interior of this book is printed on paper that contains 100%
post-consumer recycled fibres, is acid-free, and is processed chlorine-free.

16 15 14 13 12   1 2 3 4 5

Library and Archives Canada Cataloguing in Publication

Moritz, A. F.
The new measures / A.F. Moritz.

Poems.
Also issued in electronic format.
ISBN 978-1-77089-110-4

I. Title.

PS8576.O724N43 2012   C811'.54   C2011-908575-5

Library of Congress Control Number: 2011945343

Cover design: Bill Douglas
Typesetting: Alysia Shewchuk

We acknowledge for their financial support of our publishing program
the Canada Council for the Arts, the Ontario Arts Council, and the Government of Canada
through the Canada Book Fund.

Printed and bound in Canada

MIX
Paper from
responsible sources
FSC® C004071

ANCIENT FOREST ™
FRIENDLY

THE NEW MEASURES

TABLE OF CONTENTS

The Book to Come / 1
Simplicity / 2
The Location of the World / 3
Ascent of Man So Far / 4
The Snake / 5
The Hand / 7
The New Measures / 8
Full Circle / 10
The Idea of the Flood / 14
The Volcano / 15
Explorer's Notes / 17
Eve / 18
Song: How Softly It Rains... / 20
My Hero / 21
Fukushima Dai-ichi Psalm / 23
Symbolism / 25
The Cold: a Testament / 26
Voice as Time, World, and Presence / 28
The Stranger / 30
View from and of an Airplane / 31
Riding West in Autumn / 32
At Erie / 33

Farm Engulfed / 34
Farewell to Lake Michigan / 35
Pond in November / 36
The Grand Narrative / 37
Essential Poem / 39
Vista Completely Filled In / 40
Noon in Our World / 41
The End of Osiris / 42
The Good Listener / 43
The Visible Brother / 45
Painting and Poem / 46
City Center / 48
The Spoken Word / 50
Child in Fountain / 52
Woman Turning a Corner / 53
In the Food Court / 54
The Soliloquy / 56
Analysis of a Dream / 58
News / 59
Open House / 62

Notes and Acknowledgments / 77

THE BOOK TO COME

Each page in this book is first. Each re-begins
everything the others had decided
once and for all—"Behold, I make all things new"—
and happy, forgets the others
ever were. It sets out at naked dawn
in culpable but perfect innocence,
joys in the terror of stumbling on alone,
grows sick of the perpetual recurrence,
eternal return to childhood,
the endless concourse of fresh days: nothing
but uninhabited wealth and being free
and needing to make it a world. Each longs to be
one worker among many, a happy piece
in a progress—longs for a mature
continuity, a classic harmony of measured
stages completed and preserved, dross purged
and the pure sums added, the clear results
amounting to a city held in a single glance.
In that splendid extent each page trudges lost
and when it stumbles, startled it comes on words
of another there before it—"Breathing in,
breathing out, o Elysium"—and sees
its hope is wrong, its glory dark, and so
crosses itself out and starts again.

SIMPLICITY

The first and simplest things were best.
Light, and then darkness and wind.
Water, which is light with darkness
for its body and wind
for its blood and action. Then trees
arise on its banks: complex things
and implying complexities, implying
a whole earth, but staying where they are,
at home to pay homage to the simple.
Trees arise and are unformed song,
whether sound when the air stirs
or the rhythm of their standing side by side
in silent black or bright. Next comes one
traveling, eager, a dread of what comes next,
who stops under them awhile,
imagines their lyrics, and imagines
himself abolished in simplicity.

THE LOCATION OF THE WORLD

I think that in the interstices
in my sobriety, an expanse
like a humid night with lightning
or a dry poisoned ground or a concrete wall
and their veins of narrow cracks,
I am almost insane. And that madness
is a cool summer rarely recalled
or a cool episode of an unbearable summer, one night
where the light of the west delayed under the oaks
and spread through your hair and eyes and around your temples,
not wanting to descend from there
even into the valley of the moon
and its transformations. A time, a flower
too tiny to be known to anyone—
when I ask its name, there's a blank
silence and I too forget I ever had it
in my eyes, almost my hands,
growing from the rare fissures.

ASCENT OF MAN SO FAR

I'm sick of singing the song of the wall
and the lookout on the wall and the waiting room
with the one who waits, left alone there, fingering
the strange instruments that correspond to nothing
human but bafflement — left by a god? a monster?
a doctor of alien music, medicine, or torture?
The song of who will be coming
if anyone — the song that might be a foretaste,
a prophecy, a delusion. A certain prolepsis
based on a certain analepsis: you were here,
I seem to see, so when I say you will come,
it's time you came, it could be true. I'm sick
of being the saint in the song who reads
the primary howl, the basic rhythm
as a mode of presence, and the polyphonic critic
who reads as a mood of absence. And these mated lyrics
arise simultaneously like a trick of doves
fountaining and twisting upward, two black lines
of uncoordinated ink and blood that make a scribble
smutching the pure surface to smoke damage, smoke night —
the surface that was, I think, simple song,
that may have been earth, sky, and water,
and air that wasn't wind for once, just gentle motion
as of blood contained, not spurted out,
a breath that stayed around your forehead,
desperate to join its motion to
the stirring rings of your hair.

THE SNAKE

When you said no to me I lived two years in hell
and then came out again and walked the streets like anyone,
disproving the doctrine that the inferno's closed,
no redemption there. It has an open door of passing time
but the resurrected carry it inside as fading scar
and predestined resting place. So it was for the snake in Eden.
The hideous one became this snake, leaving hell behind
to crawl in flowering grasses, gleam on granite shelves,
sleep in a grotto, go out and sip a spring
fresh as the first dawn, which happened every day,
and not even waylay the rabbit, for this was Eden,
before the time when there was any need. It's good
to be a snake, to feel your firm length and thickness
under the purring, licking sun, to feel your body write
an S across the loam and not know there is "S"
in some realm of untouchable forms and painful
grasping and not grasping them yet to be invented.
To be all agility, muscle robed in its own power
taking on flesh of rose and gold brocade. To breathe
and split your hide and grow, keeping the same eyes,
but skinned now, with everything a greater glory that had seemed
supreme glory before—to keep your perpetual eyes
open, open all night, all day, and with your tongue
observe, enjoy the shapes and motions of heat
as a hawk sees valleys and ridges below him, as a god
watches the waves of centuries. It's good to be with your dry body
all around a human woman, your head erect and alert
before her sex, contemplating the darkness under the rosy
plumpness and light fur, like a warm stone with lichen,
thinking you could go in, while your coils—a hundred fingers

that are all one limb—stretch out between her hips,
around one thigh, across her back
to circle a breast and the neck, and your pointed tail
comes almost to rest in, almost to tickle, her navel.
It's good to be a snake, yet horrible too,
to have no arms, a mummy wrapped alive,
a man used to freedom, the shape of the human body,
but bound around now with heavy ropes
and left to lie for the coming of the torturer,
helpless forever, no hand to lift himself, to wave,
to push back pain—a cylindrical bulk
of cloud carried west, the furled withering tube
of a fallen hollyhock flower, a bowel torn out, pulsing...

THE HAND

I sing in the absence of disaster.
And the absence is a stockade without a fence,
safe little enclosure of boundless danger
to the animal that runs
everywhere, mountains, meadows, woods and waters,
the fiery upper air, and pauses to wander,
bowing the neck to the flowering grasses
that strain up to his teeth and
to the mouth of stars: shadow—a gate, and a trail
vanishing in and in.

The absence is a frame not frame
for a picture that likes to expand to the four
corners, quarters, oceans, and winds. Even the light
on the face of the picture
and the unpainted weave at its back
are part of an open frame
for the desire of color to run
to earth's center and up past space.

Tomorrow—its coming—its closing—its hand.
But disaster is not yet here. Untouched
for the moment I sing in the absence.
The perimeter doesn't exist. The sun shines

on endless eastern waters, shines overhead,
shines on the western waters, darkness comes,
its low globes shine, and then the shining sun
on the eastern waters. Nothing escapes.

THE NEW MEASURES

Metropolis, great salt mother, don't be angry
we've left you, a hive
of empty paper cells exposed, a speckle
in the scream of the dry tree.
From up there you could see,
if you could see, and pity
our dewinged march in the new mud. If we
in fact are more than one now.
If we are even three, the man and the following
woman and their lugged child, maybe dead,
on the plain without feature. Depending on the strength
of the sucking ooze from spot to spot,
their feet fall lighter or heavier
and shifting cadences occur,
arousing memories that forbid but can't prevent
nostalgia: tempi of the marches
of great armies go on for three, four steps,
then fall into the pattern
of naked boys and girls—io! io!—
treading a dance at a wedding,
three or four steps, and next the thunder meter
of vast herds, then quickly a swinging stomp
of dosido-ers on a straw-dusted pine plank floor, the beat
of runners in stadia of mown grass,
the wedding dance again, an erotica, the armies,
feet on subway stairs, long pulses
of the strides of skaters…limping of wheels,
click, click-click of a paper clip dropped
and caught in the works of a fan, the wheeze-whistle
of loosening belts in old motors…brief riffs,

mordents, crushed notes, grace notes appearing,
winks of accent in the plod...
                                        the last
of the hurl-burrl of the great city
that likening itself to a sea seemed
about to produce an inhuman music:
unvaryingly various, the surge and swell of our bodies
in unequal ranks breaking on each other,
lapsing together. To this we thought
we'd come the way we used to come to the shore
in the dark and pose our backs against
a cold fallen column of driftwood and listen
to the income and output of the ocean
in its bounds, at our feet—one who threatened
to destroy us and promised to continue
and so we were lulled
to power through those nights of ours
of sodden or dewy tiredness. But all of that broke
on the scurry of strait streets,
a wave, a dawn, an execution,
and I promise you, mother, we never did leave,
we love you,
it's simply that one morning we were gone.

FULL CIRCLE

i. m. Northrop Frye

A bell woke me and I went out
into the squares
where bells
harried men and women and were harried
by ropes, by motors.
In crossings at factories, apartments,
stores where the sun, first to work,
was starting to polish
dusty windows and goods
and wet down the pavement with light, in the plaza
of city hall, the bells' round mouths
drowned in machine noise,
their flower-chalice bodies invisible
up in masked towers, where many
in fact were recordings over loudspeakers,
reminiscences of bells
of simplified vibration and much greater power
than the old metal. But in the quiet
university common the carillon
eddied clearly in tree crowns amid wings
through brightness that hadn't yet reached the ground,
while under it boys and girls flowed
anxious and laughing in contradictory streams,
and parted around the shuffling
cancerous old scholar, intent
on each detail, the girls, the boys, the morning
flies on new roses, as he meditated
words with power. How impossible

for these bells not to toll for me
identically every morning, noon, and night,
and how hard not to hear them
harking back
to what awaits, repeats,
how hard not to hear them every time transformed
although the same. The alarm clock
rings, sentencing to the strict
day that will run you through its course,
remorseless—how hard not to say,
awake at last and settled to the yoke,
joyous in the sweat of your face,
the bell rang release
from blackness, uncontrollable
visions, desires without answer, the closed
solitary body and unvisited house
swelling with their wastes. How glorious
to be recalled from that, to be
a citizen, a layman, one of the *idiotes*
harried in the squares by the bells ringing
birth, wedding, labor
and worship, danger, dirge,
all the solemn, iron, and merry worlds
of the circle-mouthed, ever accurately
foretelling bells. And then
to say on this new day
the same things, but different, reversed and new.
Until at dusk in the exhausted crowds
you are routed across the city
by quiet bells and driven back
home. Or at last released
from death struggle
against invincible day and all the vile

merciless others, to build up
in the deep recess and seclusion of thought
a harmonious world, your gift.
But aren't you sick of always
coming back but sensing you've arrived
at a higher
or a lower point: because memory
decays and so you can't compare,
can't tell if this is a corresponding
but other place or the one
you've reached ten thousand times?
Memory fails. Thus kindly nature
shelters us, maybe, granting
a little of the comfort
of senility to our young years,
so that we can't see clearly
the unraveling of the person
loop and spiral down, tangling strangely,
with the unraveling
loops of earth—not quite in perfect
order but in principle
predictable. I wanted
a bell heard once and not again:
not forgotten but truly never
heard again. No order. To go on
to new things, not the old made strange
by evolution or oblivion. To go on
not even to heights
that must become the base
of another ongoing—these repetitions—
but in one motion continuous
and never the same, unknown. But this
is an old want, familiar—how hard it is,

maybe impossible, not to come
full circle. And a flight
without up or down, evening or morning,
is a fall: a flight that repeats a fall,
endless but not endless. It comes to
a halt in the titanic city
and its countryside all paved over
with congealed fire. There the bells wake
the lonely citizens after sleep
and shepherd the beaten crowds to sleep.
But you are always tired.

THE IDEA OF THE FLOOD

Scum of life on the ponds
clearing as it dies off in autumn
so they will stare up, bright, black and still
amid the last crumbs—a few towers
of leather, copper, and flame—of the first wonder
of the world. Many eyes with one gaze
waiting for never to rise. The angel
who brought us the idea
is always here, nude winter and summer,
unmovingly wandering in the fields and weeping by the stream
under the willow tree, whether they are fields,
stream, and willow, or later desert. The angel
is always right here, as we are,
when the sun and the planet swing away
and leave us in black space. We make
love to the angel ceaselessly,
monotonously: the body
all sex and every sex with no insides,
our love that never moves
while we desert and revolve.

THE VOLCANO

This was the earth at last. The volcano
pluming in the distance, white at its lips
that etched a kiss's shape into the sky,
brown on its shoulders with dead lava,
green toward its base. To see it rise
brought back, wound and healing,
the presence of the anthill so long buried
in our memory: buried with our five-year-old
seeing that once admired it. We lay at the tree's base
and watched each moment in the come and go
of the red ants: the scissoring mandibles,
nervous antennae swiveling every way,
the dragged burdens of white wing-scraps, the crossed paths
of two or three, confusions, turnings back, small wars,
and the constant crumbling of the hill: tumblings
of pale gold grains, dislodged
by the workers' footfalls, down the slope
from the black hole at the summit all day long
absorbing and divulging ants.

                              We recognized
then what we know: our earth today
fails to be earth, and yet in every touch
of my fingers and your hair, childhood's touch
in grass and shade still feels itself, so yes,
today is still the earth. And now we're there again
with everyone we remember. In the weakness
of the men and women of today
we remember not many: back to our grandmother,
no farther. But she's with us, she remembers

her grandfather, so he's there too, and his
grandmother, since he recalls her. And she
recalls her mother, and what makes us laugh,
now we recall her too — her lap, the shadow
of her breasts, her clothes and colors, and the soil,
roots and stems, the stamens and pollen of the flowers
of her scent. Then, dead two hundred years
in our delusion, she kisses us and says, "Children,
this is my father, you've never met him,
I haven't seen him in a long long time."

EXPLORER'S NOTES

I came to another ruin and fell into a dream.

The drums of fallen columns, terraces of the grasshopper,
and a few standing: dry trees. The crumbled volutes,
dry watercourses of ancient rains.
And frozen scrolls, horns of petrified rams.

But this is nothing, I thought, but a dream,
an aggrandizement of my childhood house
and my boy's way of talking.

Who is
this lost in the middle of his saying?
I'm lost again in the middle of my saying

the whole ruin, a vast Athens
and only a modest house in shaded Ohio
calm, sparkling in the stable sun,
founded on the receding edge, the breaking
black bubbles of the shuddering drawing out
of wealth into twilight...

the whole ruin, the modest house, was vivid again.
The phlox beds beat with blood.
The lilac by the back door, back from the dead,
rose more firmly and fell more slowly
than any fountain...

EVE

The freedom of imagination is
a matter of the weather—the inner
and the outer weather. Is it possible
to sing of summer in the winter,
spring in autumn? Your beard
and brows encased in wind-born ice, your face
a vanished race's famous statue...
to look at the three sparrows plumped and shivering
in a cedar bush, sole and rifled cottage
against the horizontal howl,
fails to reveal if in their hearts is the image
of a better time or only the ongoing
of an engine not yet off. The prayers
of Eve, who once talked with God, are similar.
She who went naked through the day and night,
inspired a lust that was the pith of cleanness,
bathed in the river and the seeing of the sun,
patted the phallus eels and fishes
and the tiger's nose, her shut-up
house now stinks of her urine, she can't smell it,
can't taste, can hardly hear, moans out
her son's name, "Abel. Abel. Abel,"
till the old man comes halting
with ruined back to try to lift
and clean her. It would be better, he thinks,
right now to be being murdered
out in the clear air, an unseen blow
and darkness, freedom, as my smoke ascends
among the timothy, in the summer scent.
My brother, where are you to share

my burden, my mother? And he went through
this and later died wifeless,
dupe of a pornographic dream, a girl
naked all the day and night. His grave is there
under the high chain-link topped with barbed wire
that runs endlessly across that lush
empty country, where on the other side
metal has never been, will never be discovered.
The overgrowth of wild grape vines,
junk trees, and milkweed makes the fence
a perfect screen and beyond it
he sited the parkland where she played.

SONG: HOW SOFTLY IT RAINS...

How softly it rains and how well
my nakedness understands it.

I was perfect alone in the sun,
o my son who loves the rain,
o my daughter who loves the rain.

My heart stammers with excitement,
the soft rain rolling down
on my face, chest, and sex.

How my nakedness understands it.

Wet leaves and petals now
are eyes, hands, and feet for me.
These are tears and this is pleasure.

My breath and pulse skip and stop,
human at last with the vanishing
visit of the rain.

O children of my children, how well
my nakedness understands it.

MY HERO

You won't find her except
wasted with the passion
and precision of the stars. Like tramps
they escape the formula
you've written for them, that describes their wanderings
perfectly. It is no prophecy,
dogs and roses say; it is prison—
but they'll live free in the corners
it predicts they'll roll to: ashes or voids
but living. What do you know about the misery
of the furious stoppage they come down to?
The desolation of poetry? It bathes in
their feelings never to be repeated,
the way her lashes bathe in the desolation
of her eyesight—lashes and sight of the beginning
and end of earth, never to be repeated, hers alone,
one only for everyone who dies lost
in the myth of roofs and caves.
The only prophecy is
endless gardens in the one ember. She went
through a thousand lovers—each of them lost—
to find a lover to be lost with,
a universe or fountain in a house
in a slush of houses
from an ant-queen abdomen
of a planet all one city. In that heap
no letter can be delivered
except by chance
word comes to everyone, a favorable evidence,
or in some domiciles, maybe all,

there is a unique immobility,
an unexampled silence,
a dead defiance with her face.

FUKUSHIMA DAI-ICHI PSALM

The land's so full of ex-life, drop a kernel
and it has to nestle in some dead man's chest
and play the part there of a new heart.
The angel in the machine, but so alive
there's nothing of it that can touch
the corruption. An almost immaterial drop,
though it encloses in its tacit shell
a universe set to explode, shining through
its suffocation down there with the light of
suns to come on corn tassels and dew. Nowhere
but skeletons to receive our seed anymore
and so the corpses blossom. But they don't blossom,
it's just the corn in their spleen. Hello,
Roger and Abigail, we want to say,
looking the head-high stalks in the face—
have you come back this way?
Talk to me. Don't just beam and nod
with the old nonchalance
I remember now—your new body
brings it back sharply—you were always an enigma to me.
If I tear off that grin of yours and shuck it
and your wet leaves squeak and your wet
hair sticks to my palms, between my fingers
with that sweet smell, summer and youth
rotting alive—will I know you then?
When I strip the kernels with my knife blade
and my thumb's pressure, and eat those seeds silent
and isolate them in my stomach from the ground
so that only in the mill of me
will they ever grow. When I hold the white stripped cob

like a piece of bone detached. I remember marrow
and used to like to suck it: "the sweet
marrow," it was called, and promised
more than it gave. The bone appears
a kind of scaffolding
on which hangs the appearance of a tree.

I'll tell you, corn, I'm afraid
of the radiation. And yet one dies
in a brace of years, or a year,
or a clutch, a convulsion, of months.
The skin, burnt by the invisible, quickly
curls away from the muscle,
paint flaking on a wall,
and elsewhere flesh grapples bone
for a long career in a green valley. I think
of a still living baby
clinging to a dead mother
in a civil war. Whatever one can't avoid
standing, one stands, and for some reason
some of us still respect the imprecation
against the death by one's own hand.

SYMBOLISM

This cob of corn—is this
your transformation,
your earth-change? Having
eaten you, do I
hold you again? Did
you drop into the land
as a seed to come forth
a blade of grass
like a tree, with kernels
that are teeth, cool
close-packed suns, drops
of a golden ocean,
nuggets of sugar? And
can I talk to the blackbirds
and the spiders that
cling to you, making you
some part of their worlds,
as if they are syllables
meant in friendship and
gathering to a sentence
intelligible to me? You
are dead and this life
doesn't satisfy. It
seems to me I'm alone
if sometimes happy to be.

THE COLD: A TESTAMENT

As I sit here, the sun almost gone out,
chattering on this earth where nothing's left
for me to burn, no wood, coal, oil,
no ruins whether on or in the ground,
everything already cannibalized,
I'm happy. I've read all their helpless books.
Who else ever had the time for that?
And my amazement far surpasses theirs.
In their lush world, the light on mulberry leaves
and shadow patterns of the smashed mauve berries
staining the concrete sidewalks baffled them,
and what a girl did in showing off her thighs
and why a boy's heart and breath would stop as though
for death at the sight. But I had the arabesque,
the endless curlicue, filigree, brachiation
of their words, thoughts, and feelings, denser than
the jungles they knew and their crowds of waists and eyes,
all long gone. They were prophets too. They looked
forward and pitied me. The last man. "Apocalypse"
they called their baring of future, truth, and death,
as if the very nature of the mouth
leads to sorrow, a song of empty aisles,
and one left there, who will have, for when he dies,
only the cold as help and ceremony.
But I love my poor world. I'm here. I'm glad
they didn't smash the earth to void their fear
of the long slow decay. I'm glad I had
my shivering, lonely childhood. And one day,
exactly like they did, I'll fall asleep for the last time
and dream those near-death dreams—first love,

parents alive once more, a long walk
through the skies. The dreams that come as sleep
perfects itself. The cold will give me dark
for warmth and comfort. The cold is not so bad.

VOICE AS TIME, WORLD, AND PRESENCE

When the last page of the scriptures
blows down the street, watched by sausage strings, rust-colored
    fedoras,
and sunset glints in broken glass…When it blows along
accompanied by page seven of a newspaper
from thirteen years ago, school levy narrowly defeated…
When they skitter together but apart
like two dogs, nosing into corners, sticking,
then running on…Was the last page
torn out in despairing anger or saved to cling to, to hold
next to a heart, before an eyeball? Did the last man
cherish it, spit on it, or is it a random ash, from when he went out
on his back lawn to read the holy book and the funnies
in shades and shorts, at ease on his chaise longue
of aluminum tubing and plastic upholstery, ready to receive
a tan from the bomb burst before the blast wave approached
and his body exploded like a dry tree when a wildfire
creeps close down a slope? In any case, Lord,
put an arm around my shoulder, now that I'm alone.
Let me feel your hand, see your eyes. Don't tell me
if I need a sign I'm a faithless generation. No question
of faith remains. I'm alone. I need your voice
human in my human ear, the way I heard
my lover's words. Not a story to be recalled
but a story continued day by day ever varied:
the heaven of her wisdom I would try, I swore,
to remember forever. Then she was gone and it faded
day by day. Her words, her ideas gone, only the tone
of love remaining. And then the tone too gone.
Only a sense we had talked once day by day,

a knowledge of heaven stretching back to the dawn
of my earth. Although destroyed it remained,
a beautiful homeland if only I could reach it.
A conversation, the hearing of the clear voice
of another once in the cool air, words that became,
it's true, a legend later when they faded,
but the voice never: now and always it went on.

THE STRANGER

I knew I could enjoy the stones forever,
the ocean whispering on my left, and green wet lamp-fruits
of seaweed—disembodied organs, hollow and split—
and white wood bone-forms all around.
Proud in their varied ovoids, the stones were dark
and soft, of a frigid warmth, heaped and distinct,
some crossed by lines of chalk and rose
or caravans of stipples,
and any one I touched and turned, how, pointing,
pointing and licking, touching, the light
like a faithful guide and tactful lover
compelled me to praise, moved and taught me wonder
across its skin, traveling the tranquil scars, the dimples
and spaces between features. One I remember
all black but for a burning, silver-dun
sprinkle of old stars, and a subtle ring-shaped ridge:
along this rim the noon's light shone redoubled,
like the sun condensed into the fiery
eyelash of eclipse light. Large and small,
magnificent and dull, the stones lay tumbled
on and under one another, and I trudged,
head turning here and there, hands lifting,
stroking, and dropping bodies, my eyes
looking back drunk on volumes and colors,
in a fallen city where no one halted me.

VIEW FROM AND OF AN AIRPLANE

I don't know anything.
But birch grove, cedar, pine tree, oak, and maple,
and four-stemmed fountain
of an elm surmounting all,
free of motion, translating the light stir
of the cool day in a vision
subtle in its greens, toward the south golden,
to the north a darkness of central forests
brought out and held in the sunny air in the form
of that one isolated tree. The space
among the trees is what goes by the name of silence
and emerald levels of a slope
are the dream of the dreamed river that calmly
runs upstream, leaving the sea,
and climbs the waterfalls to find…
to reach again…Light passes
down the mazes of needles and leaves
to stop and sleep here and there as white
patches on trunks, like laborers
or maybe tramps thrown down sleeping
on the rifted soil
of rich and complex fields
in a hill country. Polished magnolia,
birch grove, cedar, pine tree, oak, and maple,
the four-stemmed fountain of an elm
and the space among: eternity
in the heaven of my skull, and also
nothing—a moss-hued scrap not even
glimpsed by an eye that maybe loves the moss—
in the heaven of that airplane passing over.

RIDING WEST IN AUTUMN

A horizontal rain of silver drove but floated
for hours along the windows as the train
rhythmed west: stars, ropes of stars, flicks and flaws
of down from fountain grasses, goldenrod, and thistles…
it may be that I never should have given
an explanation, should have left an apparition,
rain of silver, unreferred
to the logic of earth. This fleece
blew in a westerly wind we couldn't feel,
encased as we were in the cars and the wind of our speed
and hurled against it. The seed
arose from white gold stubble
on embankment slopes and became in the air
silver, and the light in the big clear windows,
motionless in the rush, grew silvery too,
an ever darker silver. It was November,
by late afternoon we'd hurried into the region
too dark for reading by the sky. The lamps came on
and then our faces appeared in the glass
and our gazes turned to our laps.

AT ERIE

Clutch of five empty shells,
bivalves loosely and firmly
clinging together dead,
swinging from one another, bells
with clappers gone…or charms
for a wrist of air, or split grapes or open
beaks in a nest. The whole community
(back to back, cheek to cheek, one
for all and all for one) fits in between
the base of a man's ring finger and his line
of Venus: the whole small ruin, five
clean halls abandoned. Silent roofs.
Empty eye sockets with at bottom
still deeper dimples: little wells
that look, look back, and seem
for a second like pupils. Open doors,
open gates of a people who built
in whorls, ellipses, severed cones
and then went where, leaving the echo
of mead joy in the smooth circlings
of their bone-huts. The colors of dawns
and cold winds, different day by day,
across the cloudy lake echo divine
pleasure they sucked in moments
of safety and enough, a contented
sluggish drunkenness that was more
in the wine of the water that moved them
than in themselves, more in the light
that dried and withered them away
than in themselves.

FARM ENGULFED

I got up in the early twilight and went out
when everyone else it seemed was watching television
or driving up and down on Vienna Road,
and hooked the watering trailer to the small tractor.
I filled the black tank, turned on the modest clatter
of the engine, and drove out into the sunflower field
west of the house. The moisture darkened the gray
dust and clods, and the big wheels of the tank
waddled behind me over the uneven soil
so that the spray-bar's ends dipped and rose
like a rope walker's pole. The birdsong—oriole,
robin, bluebird, and cardinal—is always eclipsed
by the start-up of the engine and is louder
when it shuts off, clearer in a stiller sky,
a higher and darker light. But the old machine
helps with the dry month—gives the hissing
of water, and sprouts the smell of rain-wet ground.

FAREWELL TO LAKE MICHIGAN

Put your hand into my side, the oak said,
the full moon in his May crown. My love and I were leaving
the shore of Lake Michigan as a home forever
although we swore we'd come again
over and over, wraiths in the paths where strangely
we would not meet ourselves—as if belovèd
returnings for years had failed to carve our mark there
deeply enough. I'd gone out to the bluff
to visit the oak a final time, my friend,
in his pride of place in Olmstead's paradise
along and above the monster of frigid energy,
paradise itself for the invulnerable eye to play in
immensity and change. I circled him. My hands
were on his bark, my eyes in his filtered light
from lamps along the path and from the moon,
my thought part with him and part polluted
with Druids and the groves of Dodona, but trying
to be pure of knowledge. As if I could memorize
his form and body in my spine, so the image
of my skeleton and nerves would branch and leaf in me
and my body blossom in the world. Was this,
it struck me, the return of cryptic mysticism,
or a radical democracy, tree and man free equals?
Then: "A rebirth of mysticism," he said,
"is the one way to a complete equality."
This is just my translation of light and shadow
along his trunk, the subtle panoply
of his night grays, the cold roughness of his skin
on my hands: the words of his inner mass, the flow
he's carved in. But an accurate translation.

POND IN NOVEMBER

Beauty in cheerlessness—
the steadily bluer harder brighter
glance of a pond in late fall
not quite frozen yet, glittering
a stone awareness
in long fields white and gold
that lap the barn and house
in fit vestments for this
lying in state of theirs: closed walls
of such a calm it may as well be
eternal. True twilight of 3:30,
sun as low southwest
as southeast the moon is,
a ghost that pauses to be seen
and so believed in. But no ghost:
a gauzy shellfish, nearly dead,
translucent with age and strain
and crawling too slowly to betray
motion, or dead already and lying
on that blue beach where it always lay
but now lit up—a paler birthmark
in a glowing waste, with the sun
still lower now and the pond copper
crossed by richer copper and old leather
echoes of the trees.

THE GRAND NARRATIVE

The waters of the pool were troubled
each day, but only at the certain hour,
evening, when the angel entered—
when light, newly reaching
the beginning of its fading,
was most powerful, least dazzling, wholly
absorbed in colors. The water
cured every sickness in the first who touched it
and the blind man stretched out close by
and no one ever told him
the turbulence had come and the city
was darkened, the end had passed
but not yet fallen. No one
so much as kicked him so he tipped
into the boiling, into the seeming
the flat dusty pond was about to be
a fountain. Teacher, he shouted once,
when he heard the teacher had come,
there's no one to carry me to the pool,
and the man answered him: Here.
Here is an inexhaustible
troubling. It's yours now. You can
see and walk. Remember me
next time you're lame, blind, gnarled,
stuck in anemia or filth. Enter
the memory and see
the world shine
hating you, filling you
with beasts and birds, trees and flowers,
the growing distant

gabble of many friends, and walk
to unjust death in this city, this
happiness of living and moving again.

ESSENTIAL POEM

for John Hollander

Although it's likely you're on your own
(at this moment in this city of five million)
reading the poems of Traherne,
and there was no one till you lit your lamp,
the kingdom of childhood keeps being founded
in his voice and his seeing,
which are a sort of birth. A birth goes on
in the dark of a poor family, or a mother alone.
Then comes the small bright circle of the faces:
lover pores over sleeping loved one, parent over child
in their enclosure we name home,
a hut in the plain so bare there's not a tongue
of grass to make the wind hiss. Unknown
to the world a world exists:
trees and streams, birds all the colors of the flowers.
So Traherne pours over you
his wild remembrance of the world to come. And would
even in the silence of his book
if it were lost and lay unopened
two hundred years. Even if he had died
before he sang the Eden in his look.

VISTA COMPLETELY FILLED IN

Looking at this fullness
what you see is
the skinny business
over emptiness:

the flab of cars and people
where the war was
and soldiers topple,
where the patients are
dragged to complete distress
deep behind walls.

It's solely their kingdom here:
the undying removals
beyond all this
appearance,
the concourse of holes
and the field of wounds
they possess.

NOON IN OUR WORLD

Time was still.
To stop that nonsense
a helicopter
beat the sky.

THE END OF OSIRIS

Members of the god? The pieces
dispersed over the earth, composing the earth,
were doing fine on their own and didn't want
or remember, for all anyone could tell,

being one. Blank dispersion. And if you said
"the parts of a shattered corpse," they all
might laugh at once. The forearm crawled
using the fingers of its hand to scratch the dust

and scrape along painfully, happily —
the piece of a malign unkillable puppet
or the amputation from a mad assassin
on the move across deserts of tile. Image

born years back in a narrated horror,
endlessly cycling now on film and so
able to pass everywhere, a radiation,
penetrating hearts where words don't go.

THE GOOD LISTENER

How often I've heard him tear himself apart
in front of me, and what was beautiful
was miserable. As in my nursing work I see
the insides of a head sometimes—like a pumpkin,
they always say, kicked and breached, the wet
pulpy meat, sticky and sickly sweet-smelling,
the lumpy slurry with its pips and fibers:
all that remains of complicated dreams
that were continuous somehow with hope:
next year's vine. Or a body is being cut
open and I help. It's hard to do, thank God,
preoccupying, because without the strain,
the horror of the wet machine behind the smooth
belly now turned to a flap would…Who made him
be so in pain inside, tangled in himself
and hating the knot, that again and again he rips
his quiet face off? It's like the shrieks and sobs
of a marriage coming out from behind a still
house front, out the windows, across the garden
and into the street, a mean gang of noises,
pathetic bullies, forcing everyone else
to cower under them—does that comfort him?
It seems as though there has to be a play
and there's nothing else he has to put on stage.
Just what's inside, but it's ugly. Ugly when
let out into the light, like a bowel or heart.
At first I felt compassion but I can't live
with my love brought down to compassion.
The image of a man as strength, a beautiful
skin over a fire, is a necessary world

even if only an image desired so much
it's worse than needed. Now that my world
has been destroyed, I'll have to find another.

THE VISIBLE BROTHER

In the prison
house of my imagination
imagination is the prisoner and inmate,
desperate, comfortable,
and imagination is the wall, the one
landscape the inmate has ever known,
and windows in the wall that show
a deep valley and the endless
revolving sky. Or are those pictures?
Moving pictures, which only means
they move us, not that there's motion there
although I feel you with me, invisible brother
who never speaks, as I walk across the field
at November's end, first day I see
every last leaf is down. On my entering
the park: a man, a poor half-cracked
man known to me by sight, confronting,
almost kissing, the smooth clear orange bark
of a naked tree. Head way back in neck-breaking
throat-proffered-to-the-murderer position,
he watches a black squirrel, glossy as a star,
in a high groin, rummaging
through the white sky. He has a friend,
oblivious, this creature. I am walking
to the doctor, maybe to the entrance
to the passage to death,
still passage in the shape
of a body outstretched between dreaming and pain,
where you withholding the power that I want
will sit by me
unknown to me and weep.

PAINTING AND POEM

Time had to be mined from the painting, the delusion
of stillness was so powerful in it.
Gem or magma, motion was frozen up,
enthralled, below its surface: the two friends
in a mild late summer evening. Their hands
have just quit touching. One of them will go
in a white skiff at their feet, out past the headland
with its cylindrical temple in the middle distance.
The woman they both love is not portrayed
except as the golden sunrise or more likely
sunset to which all lines recede, the mouth
of shadow spilling light for now. Also the light
comes from them, is the fount of their eyes and sex
turning to the west. I had to read the painting
a long time to see the poem it entraps,
trying to redeem words from fury and long time.
First I imagined it hung on a wall in a train
racing to collision decade after decade
till it became antique. The wood of the old coach
and the ties rotted, the engine and the rails
rusted, the railroad slumped into earth, the painting
remained alone hurtling ahead, a tattered
scrap of bygone taste. And why imagine a train,
I thought next. Just by hanging in the world
the painting's on that train. Its mild regretful
stasis of a perfect dying afternoon,
warm, dry, and soft, in a rich temperate land
that everyone remembers, even if he's never known it—
it's so much like those pauses where the struggle
to prosper, or survive, doesn't matter, as if we had died

and judgment had been in our favor, we'll be allowed
to re-begin our failed attempts forever
without injury, in hope. All this is plunging
into the blank forward. An invisible haste,
an unvarying acceleration, carries it
whether to wreck or wear away in the wind
who knows? And that's why there's nothing mild
beneath the image. Words scream out. A wound
of sound thickens but oozes, never quite
scarring over, or a knife too quick to be seen
re-cuts it, and it springs again. And someone
comes to stand before this over and over
and fastens the word beautiful to the fact.

CITY CENTER

The motionless light heals even the filthy wall,
the concrete of incompetence
with its gaping pores and projecting wens and warts
that grasp a miser's share of the gold
of dust as it passes in a breeze
and later use the rain, that falls
pure on the outlying orange groves,
to turn it to thin mud. But now
a noon never to pass
makes the wall burn with the power
that needs and eats no fuel
and lives forever because it does not live at all
in the eddying way. The sick wall
flowers, becomes the human sign
in the garden at the beginning. Now vines,
that were unkempt until they spread
across the wall's top edge and fell
neatly, form the image of a daughter's hair
brushed and parted perfectly and woven with pearl
and diamond threads—a daughter otherwise naked,
except for the light that resurrects the wall,
dress of a deeper nudity. The daughter: she is safety
and desire under guardian trees, although
there are no trees in the dusty downtown,
no vines, no flowers, and the women,
not young, not slender, waddle
muffled up against paralyzing light
along the frying barrenness of the wall. How good
to know this light is not unchanging, this moment
of suffocation

will never be eternal. In the illusion
of noon's stillness, the sun shifts to the west
and consumes itself, and particles shoot
into the crying brain and liver. Everything
sifts and grinds away invisibly
to the other light always unchanging
the wall and the poor banished leaves.

THE SPOKEN WORD

She says one word: "Ridge"
and you look at it
floating there alone
though it's vanished now,
has returned again
into the mind's dark
dictionary and
silence that takes back
this room and your ear.
But her saying it
still quivers, the flower
on the stalk of your
memory of her
speaking. You're a stem
connecting her "Ridge"
to the endless root
of the word buried
in language, its loam
quaking on a core
of metal on fire.
Why that one word here?
Has she gone mad? What
sentence did it leave
behind it or fly
to join, what work gang
or purgatory
of words? Who are its
wife and its brother
words, its family of
a moment, its place,

its generation,
its village of words
to give it a life,
to come before it,
last after, and be
grandparents to it,
graveyard and church bells,
and at last ghost town?
They never appeared.
It rose alone and
its "rrr" and its "dge"
were the mud on stone
of the ridges of
her native town and
its "id" was the light
of the sun rising
or setting out from
the long forested heights.

CHILD IN FOUNTAIN

The playground silent as the tomb. The swings
twist with their absent infants in a breeze
that sounds a softened ocean rolling and tossing
in the heads of locust trees, green ashes,
and the maples, their darkness flecked with hanging gold
of the year's last crop of keys. My grandson
is far away in school across the city
although it's hot as summer here. The empty
October afternoon gilds the sand and gives
a finer orange, blue, lime green, and pink
to the forgotten plastic toys that stud it
like flecks of brilliant paint suggesting flowers
across the lowest ground of whatever painting
is most primitive, most beautiful. Now is the
passing pause between crickets and the snow,
when dragonflies drift mating in warm shadows
near the red lamps, the yew berries. We two
are still in the same time, but not in the same place…
as we were when we played here in August and he swung
and dug, and in the chaos of shouts burst through
the diamonds of the fountain, now shut off,
as they fell from endless crests and turned to water.

WOMAN TURNING A CORNER

You'll disappear
and leave me in this street of the sun,
this straight way with its red ember bricks at noon,
the vertical knife edges of its walls,
where they end, cutting into a sky
the blue of life, of cold
lake water.

What will you be in that cross alley
you'll turn into, where I can't see?
But I see here,
as you approach the corner where you'll disappear from me,
your white blouse at the collar quiver
and on your nape the golden
and white hairs, a few
threads or lines that change their curve
but keep it in mind
and always return, that part
and gather in the slight wind, quiver.

And with your gait,
as you approach the point where turning
you'll disappear, the point for all I can see
only a shallow shadow on a long bright wall,
I shake
in dust and light
with the leaves of some tree
or the windows of some tower you may come to know
in that street at a right angle
beyond my sight.

IN THE FOOD COURT

I had this idea yesterday, I heard
this bird sing yesterday hidden in the foliage
of the big mirrors cladding the sides
of the square pillar in the food court
near Manchu Wok. And if I'd written it then
the words that came to clothe it would have been
different entirely, except for the first line,
I had this idea yesterday. And the lovely girl
and nearby crockery accident that sent the poem
in an unplanned direction, never to recall
its first hope — lost, all lost — would have been
different intrusions. But who knows?
Maybe today's distraction and yesterday's,
two strands of a river divided by an island
in Eden, both lead from different angles
into the same pleasure and rapids up ahead.
Whether we round the bend on the left
or the one to the right, maybe the currents
draw to the same scene. We drift past
the greening statue of a naked boy, thieving
Hermes or Cupid, who looks like me fifty years ago,
towards a flurry of white water, cataracts tumbling
down black bright rocks and sending up many
a plume, panache, fountain-shaped feather
of mist. We glide darkly under
close-woven sycamores through the constant
pregnancy of surrounding earth. The stone
and the boy's eroding sides are rich
in slimy mosses, washed in the iris
and diamond of the rising and dying *brume*

and all of this wet dark is...what? we don't have
the adequate verb—not fucked, not made
love to, something between—by the shafts
of sunlight that penetrate, and the marble
presence of the child god. Father and son,
light and sculpture, rapturous in the garden
of self-proffering femininity. Maybe the poem
never recalls but does recover
its first intention, coming with no flicker
of recognition or memory
to the place it started for long ago:
everything lost except pure joy
or the hell of energy restored to stillness:
pure joy. Anyway, yesterday
I had this idea, this line of lyrics
to put to a bird's song I heard
from the mirror boskage in the underground city.
Everything that comes has come before
but in some other, forgotten shape
that was never, or badly, born
and insists, waiting to be loved properly.

THE SOLILOQUY

Under the huge black willow still
fully in leaf in November, I found myself
saying this: the old convention
of soliloquy is perfect realism.
For there I was, muttering to myself,
part self-forgetful, part guardedly aware
not to be overheard and understood
for a lonely fool. "Soft you now!"
Ophelia passed me like a prayer, skating
on the winding paths of that park,
in this era when no one believes and she
has to be the prayer herself. I shut up
before she could hear me and fear
and she passed away and I thought:
The drama shows us buried, drowned,
shut up in each other: corporate
action, a pattern where we're threads
that lie knotted: orgiasts wrapped
in stinking gear and entangled
on the one permitted bed: millipedes
heavily cloaked by a stone in a hole.
And though the story is hatred, murder,
war, as it has to be, the pattern
never loosens: it exists, we live
tied into each other in the crisis of
mutual burning, never let be. Yet in
this dictatorship of togetherness,
the poet has shown the slender veins
of aloneness run. Has shown them broaden
to fertile valleys in that moment

when the history riots and ruins
outside a door or around a corner for once
and there's no one near—there's no one
else but a voice, your own, agonizing
to build a body, a face, a world
with itself for its only lover,
its teeth for its only orator,
its ear for its only crowd,
its vacant sorrow where it drops
like leaves in a pond
for its only city square. There it tries,
whatever it says, to satisfy
or exhaust its rage for saying
so it can be silent at last and hear
the apostle, "Brethren, let us learn
to love one another," and return
to the action changed, return
to men and women who find each other
faintly repellent—what am I saying,
"faintly"!—and see them stripped,
and lovely through nakedness not pity.

ANALYSIS OF A DREAM

The poem I want to write you is a dream
but I can't dream it with you, only tell you,
wide awake, what it was like. "You stood in a doorway
and caught my eye across the room.
I'd thought you were in India, and I came walking
through the air, above the heads of the others,
but there was something I was supposed to bring you,
a cup, or some sort of long animal
with soft rubies for fur. So I turned back
and went looking for that, worried,
not knowing what it was…" And you would think,
listening to the dream, I had a face in it, my face,
that I was only me, walking on the air
near the ceiling of that room like a mountain valley
with geometrical cave-palaces
carved into the cliffs to thousands of feet
above a flowering jungle. I got lost there
and never made it back to where you waited.
Then I woke up. So now I have to tell you:
in that dream I have no face, or not this face.
I have no awareness of a face. You look at me
as if I stir you: a human being, a man, beautiful.
When you see me, light flows out of you, your lips,
forehead, white dress, the round of hips and belly.
And I look back at you free of shame. My face
forgotten, like a child's. I'm not surprised
my face that brought me failure brings your light.

NEWS

They brought him news: the serpent had come
from its hole in the golden mud and stung
and killed his wife beside the river
as she was bathing. They came running
through the fields, tunneling the high gold hay,
making a ripple—like a breeze
or the flowing mark of a hidden snake,
its advance in the grass—which he had seen
when they were still far off. He looked
homeward from his work under his vines,
his hands still raised among the grapes
as if he were tied, they later said,
to be beaten there. His head was twisted
to his left shoulder and tipped back slightly
to lift the gaze, and the sky was cut out
by the line of his nose, lips, and chin—
a complex coast, blue sea, white shore—
and they thought of how the corpse was lying
waiting for him, naked, wet
with river as though with dew, its profile
against the dim of the hut and the rush mat.

His vines were savage, yet the sweetest.
He grew the wild grape unimproved.
Now his grainy fingers in the bunches
of the small violet dusty fruits
were like pale goldenrods gone to seed
mixed in among October asters...
but in these grapes, like a loud cry
heard once in the night so sharp and clear

that when it's gone it's not believed
by the only one who heard it, was sweetness
that made the farmers drink their envy
and strain against heaven's injustice
and feel now in their fatal news,
in their duty, a hateful satisfaction.

Then he ran home and running he saw
a walnut lying withered far
from any walnut tree, and faded,
hardly green, so that he thought it
a horse's dropping at first, but then
a walnut. He saw the pine cones, some
smashed, some perfectly unfolded.
The brown suns of the chestnuts, some
nibbled, the green-white innards bared.
He saw a mushroom, gray and crossed
by wide white causeways, and another
kicked over—saw the jagged stump
of the stem, a broken world of breakings,
like the young mountains are. He came
to the hut, bent down to the low door,
dark and small, and she received him,
happy to see him. She kissed him, the full
length of her stripped body kissed him,
the front and the back of her body kissed him
all at once. Then they went out,
forgot she was naked from the bathing,
from that interrupted making ready,
forgot the grapes too, and walked together
by the river, back the way the screams
of the women had come, into the hay
where the silent messengers had gone,

and tried to remember and tell each other
their whole day, all that they'd seen and done.

OPEN HOUSE

I

They started with a question:
how could they unlock their door
and give to everyone who asked
and still be anything themselves, still work
and have a place to offer, not fade away in the swarm
of everything that enters, driven
or simply leaking, spreading,
to wash away their outline, erase their face?

2

That's not right. They started with a jug
on a small table. A tall jug,
elegant and approximate in its symmetry
to show it was content, even proud, to be primitive,
to let its hardness and its fierceness
shine, like the eye of an animal: sad and mild.
It was shaped like an upright gourd with a beak
and bore the painting of a cock, claws spread
and screaming or crowing, at a fox or dawn.
Red, green and black were the broad slashes
that gave the cock as if alive. A handle,
like holding the wild bird by the wings. The jug
in their imagination always held beer,
or water, wine, or some modern drink,
filled with bubbles so it would wink
like fountain spume forever replenished in the basin:
whoever dared to come in would have what he wanted,
the same open abundance as the cool of night.

3

That's not right. They started with some friends.
Newly married themselves, they imagined
a house all unlocked. Many doors.
A body constantly penetrated
by lovers like a summer rain,
the kind that lightly quivering the petals
erects a wakeful night
stiller than deep sleep...and also the kind
that shivers the house and tears with its nails
to fissure the earth and work in,
and rolls over like torrential sweat
down a back about to break,
so that house and ground whirl
on a current, threatening to split in fragments
and dissolve, be part of the mire
suspended in a world a flood.

4

That's not right. These friends of theirs
were other boys and girls, newly women and men,
not a storm or a stream of sperm.
The house was an apartment: complaisant, yes,
but not a temple whore. The dream
of infinite permission and entry was a thing—
as a dream is a thing—among
their things. One of these was the world's
most comfortable armchair, pale green, worn plush
like a lawn of bluegrass with children
always playing. Two polished ducks' heads of gold wood
made the handles of the rests. It had come there
from the Salvation Army store with the other chair
where one day they'd give their son
his first infant haircut: straight cherry wood frame,
noon-blue seat but night-blue back
with a brilliant bouquet in fading needlepoint,
a permanent, almost permanent
firework of blossom.

5

The dream
of permanent openness and festival
floated over and among their other things,
bathing them, covering them in a new skin of sparkle
that was sometimes glory, sometimes loathsomeness.
They hadn't even yet unlocked their doors
but it seemed a riot of tribes
ate everything, howling without truce
and sometimes they too joined in and displayed
their own crests, dances, and intricately carved throwing sticks
with three deadly blades. They loved
the moment of tired calm, the night, the variously tattooed heads
breathing together asleep, though somewhere
a voice could be heard muttering: someone drawled a story
and maybe there was even another one
half awake to listen. In these happy isles,
before morning uncovered
the piles and scraps of filth, the breakages
of goods and bodies, a corpse or two,
a maiming cut or two, the wreckage of carnival, they saw
all brought together by their house, a world
of bodies permanently entering and accepting other bodies,
a world all one place. In these happy isles
a sad wondering would also come—
what had they been before, when they had been alone
and composed, the two of them,
an image of a loving world entire? Then the sleepers
would all rise from their universal bed,
those of them still living, those
still able-bodied, and the riot of

communion would pick up
and take over all their heart, their room, again.

It's not right. They started with ashes
of a fire that had burned down in the grate:
the words, Give to whoever asks…
Sell all you have and follow…
They'd seen this ash: beautiful huge houses
on terraces over the lake when they were invited
as an experiment by the rich, a gesture to the no ones.
Their own three rooms had an old blocked fireplace they swore then
to resurrect, and their window
looked down on the sidewalk and the thick lousy manes
of many restless lions of the art
of mumbling to the self, the oral epic
of insanity, cadging, obscene vituperation
out in the rainy air forever transforming,
by a cruel automatic magic
(once the houses of summer and fall
had demolished themselves), into the flop of ice,
desert of frozen exposure the prairies hurl
down on Lake Michigan, flattening all makeshift walls,
leaving scarcely a stone standing
to shiver behind, erasing from even that one stone
the epitaph. The corpse, hard
in the dawn of its discovery,
the daybreak of the police, a mortuary
ice sculpture the wind toppled in the dark, would have to be
its own monument. Now where is that dead beggar?
Who lets, who brings him in? What human wall,
permeable but sheltering, lets him enter through it
like a ghost and then enfolds him
back to flesh, back to gracious speech,
to response?

7

They started with their own coming
together, a nameless thing, new, that later
might penetrate the closed, confused
walls of the word love
and rebuild it. They'd sweep the littleness
of despair from the great,
who can make nothing of the ashes of nobility,
of truth that still lasts on the hearth
as charcoal, too burnt to flare again,
ruin of the idea of fuel and energy. They started
to remove the appearance of burnt ruins
from the beautiful house.

Wooden clinkers, pieces of the corpse of a tree,
tiny mountains jagged with shining faces and dull faces,
fissured and planed faces, the smooth and rough
magnificence of barren granite, cold embers like scorched
fragments of living rock, the now dead
life of pure activity—of an inner fire
that was not an image
but just fire,
not a metaphor, not a carrying across to elsewhere
but an ending of an all
in itself, in its ending itself.

These bits of charred wood they carried out
from the slumped mass of the burnt-down house
making the ground hideous, and from the fieldstone
hearth undestroyed in the shambles:
embers of two fires, equal
if they become tiny mountains in the palm
alive with a life not life, as mountains are alive,
or if they stay rubble that refers to nothing.

9

It hadn't been right, their question: how could they
avoid fading in the swarm
of everything, which enters
to wash away all outline. Doesn't every thing
dissolve? When it opens just a little, all floods in.
And it itself is part of it all, of these things
and people, drops of the deluge,
and does its part in eroding
all the rest.

        It's like a small whirlpool
on a mirror stream slowly sliding
under summer stars, bearing muted
purple and brown, gold and white
of lilies, loosestrife, ironweed, cattails, and reeds
where tomorrow at noon, clear bright gold and black,
the goldfinch and its image will hover and cling
to the tall plants that burst and bare their seeds
drifting through August. The tiny eddies you hardly see
spin and on one side augment the current's
slipping away and on their other side
contradict it, turning back upstream—
or like a fly in an airliner
buzzing toward the tail, in the direction of home.
But it has no home. Its home is now
in the bottled light of forty thousand feet.

The question wasn't right: is it possible
to open to all? They'd grown up
in the error of questions. The mark
of the question had tattooed them,
a brand displaying that they belonged
to primordial punishment
and should never be punished any more.
Everyone wore the mark
and disobeyed the prohibition.
A universal harrying, each by all,
all faces burnt
with the black sickle curve and the Black Hand spot. A hell
with one circle
and there the two of them almost forgot
they'd started out as children. They have
no question and no vision
except for every leaf they come across.
They don't know generosity but see it
being newly created
each time
they close a hungry fist on what they want.

II

They started with the child—an eagerness,
a selfish anarchy admitting all. Later
it became a word they found
and pronounced: I love you
and you are precious
in my sight. The storm that night
terrified them, beating on the boards
of the cheap apartment: their still rising house
where she had separated him and he
had separated her
from the flood. But the house
almost held. A few rusty rivers down the walls.
The lightning flashed without cease, stuttering rhythm
of a heart failing, still too passionate, rapid, greedy at the end,
and then their fear, like the sorrows of children,
turned into sleep.

          By the morning,
much of the storm had drowned in the earth.
But each drop that did survive on a leaf
in the sun, they separated
in their sight. They saw the lost ones
gone into the mouths of plants, the dry dust,
the mass of water. All passersby
were resting in their house of a seeing
they could foresee. Somewhere now
the dead who had found no place in last night's storm
were being discovered.

Here's the wood thrush dead in their garden,
here's the mahogany beetle that lit in her hair,
frightened them, was brushed to the sidewalk
maybe mortally hurt, and loved by them
and hoped for there—here it is
dead in the morning. Here are snail shell, cicada hull,
bluejay refined by winter to a pale blue keel in spring mud.

Here's their gaze like children—it's curiosity,
is it sorrow, dread, a mere wonder not yet anything,
even hunger and fear? Their sight
too weak, their house too small
to take in these who are gone.
And here's their seeing
another sight, great enough.

13

So later they went out. Left the house open.
On the path through the fields alone together
they'd live forever with the amber dragonflies,
the black moths mating in air
above the brome nodding, near the birch flickering,
a fountain of constellations, in the go and come
of light wind. They'd walk with their absent friends
alone together
trying to open,
each in the house of a body
that would be all doors.

NOTES AND ACKNOWLEDGEMENTS

Thanks to the editors of the publications in which some of these poems previously appeared: *The Fiddlehead*, *The Hamilton Stone Review*, *The Literary Review of Canada*, *Micolo's Barbershop / La peluqería de Micoló*, *Poetry* (Chicago), *Riddle Fence*, *Studio*, *The University of Toronto Quarterly*, and *The Best Canadian Poetry in English 2011* (Tightrope Books), ed. Priscila Uppal.

The Book to Come
   Le livre à venir, title of a book (1959) by Maurice Blanchot on *Un coup de dés*.
   "Behold, I make all things new…" Revelation 21:5
   "Breathing in, breathing out, o Elysium…" Czeslaw Milosz, "With Trumpets and Zithers", l.4, *New and Collected Poems 1931-2001* (2003), p. 225

Ascent of Man So Far
   The Ascent of Man, title of a book and television series by Jacob Bronowski

The Idea of the Flood
English title of, and phrase from, a poem by Rimbaud which stands first in *The Illuminations*.

Farm Engulfed
Vienna Road in Niles, Ohio, is pronounced with a long i, not a long e, in the first syllable.

Essential Poem
The poems of Thomas Traherne (1637-74) were unknown (they appear not have circulated, or only narrowly, in his own time) until 1903, when the manuscript of them was discovered by scholar Bertram Dobell and attributed to Traherne by Dobell's research.

The Soliloquy
"Brethren, let us learn to love one another..." 1 Peter 1:22

Open House #1
"...give to everyone..." Luke 6:30

Open House #11
"I love you and you are precious in my sight...." cf. Isaiah 43:4
"...their fear, like the sorrows of children, turned into sleep...."
Hölderlin, "Dem Sonnengott" ("To the Sun God"), ll. 10–11

My thanks to Ken Babstock, who was deeply involved in shaping the book and many of the poems, so that *The New Measures* is in important part a dialogue between us; to T., for equally basic, crucial discussions and perfectings; to the Anansi poetry board, Karen Solie, Adam Sol, and Jared Bland; and to Sarah MacLachlan and all at Anansi for their help and welcome, which make Anansi a cherished literary home for me.

ABOUT THE AUTHOR

A.F. MORITZ has written sixteen books of poetry, and has received the Guggenheim Fellowship, and the Ingram Merrill Fellowship, and has twice been a finalist for the Governor General's Literary Award. He lives in Toronto.

79